JEET KUNE DO

JEET KUNE DO

Volume 2

COUNTERATTACK!
GRAPPLING COUNTERS
AND REVERSALS

By
Larry Hartsell
and
Tim Tackett

Disclaimer

Although both Unique Publications and the author(s) of this martial arts book have taken great care to ensure the authenticity of the information and techniques contained herein, we are not responsible, in whole or in part, for any injury which may occur to the reader or readers by reading and/or following the instructions in this publication. We also do not guarantee that the techniques and illustrations described in this book will be safe and effective in a self-defense or training situation. It is understood that there exists a potential for injury when using or demonstrating the techniques herein described. It is essential that before following any of the activities, physical or otherwise, herein described, the reader or readers first should consult his or her physician for advice on whether practicing or using the techniques described in this publication could cause injury, physical or otherwise. Since the physical activities described herein could be too sophisticated in nature for the reader or readers, it is essential that a physician be consulted. Also, federal, state or local laws may prohibit the use or possession of weapons described herein. A thorough examination must be made of the federal, state and local laws before the reader or readers attempts to use these weapons in a self-defense situation or otherwise. Neither Unique Publications nor the author(s) of this martial arts book guarantees the legality or the appropriateness of the techniques or weapons herein contained.

Book Designer: Danilo J. Silverio
Book Editors: Dave Cater and Sandra Segal

ISBN: 0-86568-081-7
Library of Congress Catalog No: 84-51053

UNIQUE PUBLICATIONS
4201 Vanowen Place, Burbank, CA 91505

Dedication

To Dan Inosanto . . .
to Gerry . . . to those I left behind
— Vietnam, 1966-67

Acknowledgements

We would like to thank JKD instructor Chris Kent; Savate instructor Salem Assli; and Inosanto Academy students Del Pollard, Tim Cardoza, Ernie Franco, Fred Brown, Cliff Stewart, Bruce Thompson, Bill Gray and Steve Connolly, for posing for the techniques in this book. Thanks also goes to Charlotte Laine for typing the manuscript.

The authors also would like to thank "Judo" Gene LeBell, who taught Bruce Lee the finer points of grappling. LeBell's tireless efforts through seminars and publications have kept the art alive.

Table of Contents

Introduction

Following the publication of our first book, *JKD: Entering to Trapping to Grappling*, we received many inquiries regarding the techniques contained therein. Because of these inquiries, we have prepared this book, which presents counters and reversals to the techniques shown in our first book. For every technique, there is a counter; for every counter, there is yet another counter. Flowing from one technique to another separates the superior from the mediocre martial artist. By flowing from one technique to another and fitting in with any opponent or style, JKD is unique among other martial arts systems and styles.

We hope the techniques presented here will encourage the reader to embark on his own path to self-discovery as a martial artist.

Joe Spallone

1 Basic Counters From The Tie-up Position

The tie-up position frequently occurs in combat. At this range, the judo, jujitsu or wrestling practitioner has a decided advantage over a boxer or a karateka. The grappler has spent a great portion of his training using techniques from the tie-up position. For him, this is where the fight starts. However, most karate or kung-fu practitioners have spent very little time working from this range. As for the boxer, at this range, he can catch his breath or clear his head until the referee breaks apart the fighters. What happens at this range will answer the question of who will win in a fight between a boxer and wrestler. If a boxer can keep a wrestler out of this range, he will have the advantage. However, if a wrestler can bridge the gap and maintain this range, he will have the advantage.

This chapter shows some possible counters to basic attacks from the tie-up position. Many of these counters are from Western wrestling and Filipino wrestling or *dumog*. Remember: There is no referee on the street!

The Single-Arm Wrap-Around

One of the techniques a boxer can use in the tie-up position is the single arm wrap-around. This technique will trap both of your opponent's arms so he will be unable to punch you.

In the basic tie-up position, both opponents grasp each other around the neck with their lead hands. At the same time, they grasp the arm around their neck near the elbow.

To get into a single-arm wrap-around, circle your front arm (in this case your right arm) clockwise. This pins the opponent's rear arm to your side.

Counters to the single-arm wrap-around

1. Small disengagement, to single-arm wrap-around, to arm-throw with shoulder-push, to elbow crank.

As your opponent attempts a single-arm wrap-around, disengage by circling your arm counterclockwise until you pin his arm to your side.

Throw your opponent by stepping in front of his front leg and twisting your body to the left as you push on his right shoulder.

After he's on the ground, control him with a figure-four elbow crank. Apply pressure by lifting up on his arm as you twist to the left.

Continued

2. Small disengagement, to neck-grasp-and-throw to neck crank.

As your opponent attempts to trap your left arm, disengage with a small counterclockwise circle while grasping your hands around the back of his neck.

Throw him by stepping to your left as you twist his neck.

Control him by kneeling and shoving his head forward with your torso.

Continued

3. Small disengagement, to wrap-right-arm. Trap left arm and hit.

As your opponent attempts the single-arm wrap-around, disengage by circling your arm counterclockwise. After pinning his right arm, grasp his left arm with your left, thus trapping both arms. Follow this with a palm to his nose.

4. Small disengagement, to wrap-left-arm. Trap right arm and hit.

As your opponent attempts a single-arm wrap-around, circle your arm counterclockwise to disengage, ending up on the inside of his right arm.

Once you have the inside line, shove his arm down as you reach through with your right. Grasp his right arm near the elbow, thus trapping both arms. Then finish him with a left vertical punch to his face.

The Double-Arm Wrap-Around

The double-arm wrap-around, which also comes from Western boxing, is executed from the tie-up position. Circle your arms until you have pinned your opponent's arms to your side.

Counters to the double-arm wrap-around

1. Double-small-disengagement, to double-arm wrap-around.

As your opponent attempts to circle his arms and wrap your arms to his side, perform a double-small-disengagement by circling your arms to the inside line. Then circle to the outside line and pin your opponent's arms to your side.

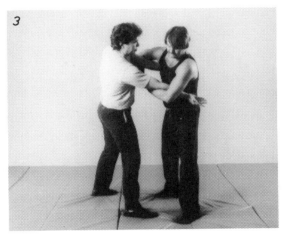

2. Double-small-disengagement to two-hand neck-grasp.

This is the same as #1, except after you've circled to the inside line, reach up and grasp his neck with both hands.

Finish him off by shoving his nose into your shoulder.

3. Front bear hug to armlock arm-throw.

Your opponent attempts a double-arm wrap-around. If you can't disengage, throw him off balance by stepping with your right foot. Hit his chest with your front shoulder as you grab him in a front bear hug.

Throw him by locking his right arm to your left shoulder. Throw him by pivoting to your right.

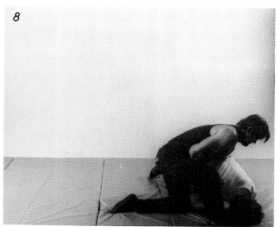

4. Double-small-disengagement with finger-jab to eye, to head butt.

As your opponent attempts a double-hand wrap-around, circle your hands to the inside line and grab him behind the neck with one hand as you jab his eye. Follow with a head butt to his nose.

Throw him with a kali *dumog* forearm drop throw. Grasp his right wrist with your left hand while placing your right forearm on top of his right forearm. Then pull up with your left hand as you push down with your right forearm. At the same time, pivot to your left.

As your opponent's falling, step forward with your right leg. Then pivot on your right and kneel on his chest and head with a double-hand wristlock.

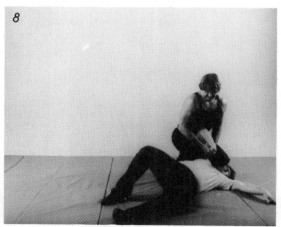

5. Head butt, to step-under-the-arm, to wristlock.

As your opponent starts a double-arm wrap-around, step forward with your right foot. Grasp the back of your opponent's neck and apply a head butt. Step under his right arm with your right leg, and lock his wrist with your right arm.

Then throw your opponent to the ground by kneeling while simultaneously pulling up on his wrist and pushing down on his triceps with your left forearm. Then sit down to execute an arm bar with a wristlock.

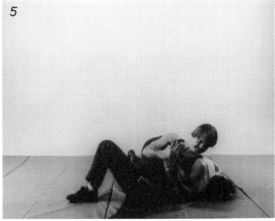

6. Head butt, to figure-four armlock takedown.

After the head butt, grab your opponent's wrist and move into a figure-four armlock. Throw your opponent to the ground by pivoting to your left as you kneel. At the same time, hit him with your right elbow.

You then can control him by kneeling on his bent arm.

Trapping Hands as a Defense for Tie-ups

Bruce Lee always felt wing chun trapping hands were an effective way to counter a wrestler. Listed are just some of the JKD trapping-hand counters to the wrestling tie-up.

1. Shoulder-shove, to pak sao and double-hit.

From the tie-up position, shove your opponent's shoulder with your right arm. Slap (*pak*) his right arm as you punch his face with your left fist. Follow up with a right punch.

2. Tan sao, to vertical punch, to pak sao-and-punch.

Circle your left hand inside your opponent's right arm. Open him up with a tan sao block as you punch with your left fist. Then pak with your right hand as you punch with your left.

3. Shoulder-shove to palm, to palm-heel to nose, to pak-and-hit.

Shove your opponent's shoulder with your right palm. Follow with a right palm heel to his nose. Then trap his right hand with a pak sao to his right arm. At the same time, punch with your left fist. Finish off your opponent with a right punch to his throat.

4. Small disengagement, to finger-jab to eyes, to pak sao-and-hit.

Circle your left hand to the inside of your opponent's right arm. Jab his right eye with a left finger jab. Follow with a right pak sao to his right arm as you punch with your left fist. Then trap his shoulder with your left palm and punch with your right fist.

5. Large disengagement to the outside, to tan-and-punch.

Trap your opponent's left arm by circling your left arm under his arms. At the same time, zone away from his right hand by stepping to your right. Shove forward with a left tan sao to pin his left arm. Then punch with your right.

6. Scoop to punch.

Circle your left hand over the top of his arms. Scoop his left elbow with your left palm, thus pinning his left arm. Then punch with your right fist.

Boxing Counters to Wrestling Tie-ups

Boxing techniques can effectively counter wrestling techniques if you go into action as soon as the tie-up occurs, before the wrestler has time to lock you up or throw you.

1. Right uppercut to a left hook.

2. Left uppercut to a right hook.

3. Left body hook to a right body hook.

4. Left uppercut to a right uppercut.

5. The six-point combination.

This is a fast series of combination punches:

a. Right uppercut to...

b. Left hook to...

c. Short overhead right to...

Continued

d. Left uppercut to...

e. Left hook to...

f. Right overhand.

Defense for Basic Pop-ups

A pop-up is a basic wrestling technique executed from a tie-up position. Below is an example of a pop-up to a side-standing strangle.

Slap up with your left palm at your opponent's right elbow. Then step up with your left leg. Bring your right forearm against his neck and squeeze.

1. Pop-up to side-standing strangle.

As your opponent attempts to pop-up your right arm, beat him to the punch by popping up his right arm. Step up with your left leg and strangle him by grabbing your right wrist with your left hand.

2. Pop-up to half-nelson, to neck-throw.

As your opponent attempts to pop-up your right arm, beat him to the punch by popping up *his* right arm. Step up with your left leg as you grasp his neck with your hand. Pull down his head by reaching under his right arm with your left and grasping his wrist. From this half-nelson position, place your left hand around his neck and throw him by kneeling as you pull.

Continued

3. Headlock to sprawl.

As your opponent tries to pop up your right arm, step up with your left leg and wrap your left arm around his neck. After getting him in a headlock, bring him to the ground by stepping forward with your left leg and sitting down.

4. Lift-arm-behind-the-neck arm-lever, to rear-leg pick-up, to leg-wrap-around-throw.

As your opponent starts to pop your right arm up, grab his right wrist with your left hand. Duck under his right arm as you step up with your left leg. Hyperextend his elbow by bracing it behind your neck. Then step behind him and pick up his right leg. As soon as his leg is in the air, step over it with your left leg. By sitting down you will have him in a bent leglock. Then reach up and pull his hair.

5. Ear-slap, to right shovel-hook, to behind-the-neck arm-lever, to kali-push-thigh-throw.

As your opponent attempts to pop up your right arm, flow with the energy he gives you by hitting him with a right backhand ear slap as you step up and to the side. Lift his right arm up as you shovelhook his stomach. Then step behind his right leg with your right, and execute a behind-the-neck arm-lever. Throw your opponent to the ground by pushing down on his thigh with your right palm. Control him by bending his elbow over your thigh.

6. Shoulder-shove to single-leg takedown, to reverse leglock.

As your opponent pops up your right arm, flow with his energy and shove him off balance by pushing his right shoulder with your right palm. Do a single-leg takedown. Then step over his leg and twist his ankle to roll him onto his stomach. Then sit down into a reverse leglock. Finish by grabbing his hair with your left hand.

Counters to the Tight Tie-up

The tight tie-up occurs when your opponent grasps your neck with both hands on the inside line.

1. Kali biceps-pinch, to elbow, to neck.

To release your opponent's grasp, reach under his left arm and pinch his right biceps. Finish him off with a left elbow to his neck.

2. Right-and-left ear-slap.

Execute a right palm slap to your opponent's left ear, and follow with a left slap to his right ear.

3. Double ear-slap, to double-thumb to eyes.

Slap your opponent's ears with both palms. Then shove him off by pushing on his eyes with your thumbs.

4. Brachial plexus nerve-pinch to overhand left.

To release your opponent's neck grasp, dig your thumb into his brachial plexus nerve. Finish him off with an overhand left punch.

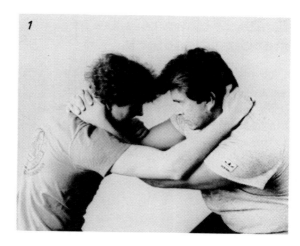

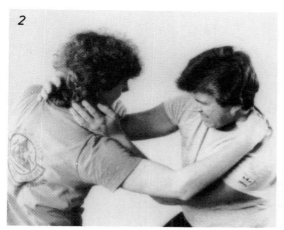

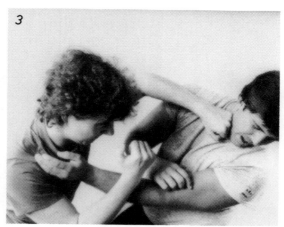

5. Elbow-down release to standing headlock.

Break your opponent's grasp by smashing down your elbow on his arm. Slide counterclockwise with your left foot and put your opponent in a headlock.

6. Muay Thai inside-arm-snake, to tight tie-up, to knee.

This counter is one of the many good Thai boxing counters. Shove your opponent's left arm out with your left hand, creating a path for your right arm to snake inside. Then grab your opponent around the neck in a tight tie-up, and finish him off with your knee.

Continued

7. Shove-elbow, to kali twisting-neck-throw, to standing armlock.

Shove your opponent's left arm to the inside with your right hand. Then switch grips by grabbing your opponent's left elbow with your left hand. Throw him by twisting his neck or grabbing his hair with your right hand as you push his left elbow. Maintain your control by bending his arm over your thigh.

Continued

8. Trap-both-arms, to uppercut, to hook, to backhand chop.

Bring your left arm over the top of your opponent's arms. Trap his arms by grabbing his right arm with your left hand. Then uppercut his stomach, hook his jaw, and backhand chop his neck.

Continued

2 Counters to Leg Attacks

Counters to the Tackle

A common streetfighting technique for the bigger or stronger opponent is the tackle. The tackle can be an effective technique for one who feels comfortable with groundfighting. To tackle someone, reach down and grab his legs while shoving forward with your shoulder.

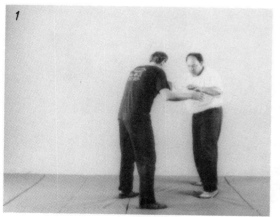

1. The sprawl with a choke.

As your opponent attempts to tackle you, step back with your right leg. At the same time, grab him around his throat with your right arm and shove down with your upper body. Then drop to the ground by stepping back with your left leg.

2. Front-choke to throw.

As your opponent bends to grab your legs, grab him around the neck, step forward with your right leg and throw him. Drop to the ground while kicking your right leg up.

3. Sidestep to the right with straight-arm throw.

Step to the right with your right foot. Then slide your left leg around as you grab his left wrist with your left hand. Throw him by kneeling as you shove down on his left arm with your right arm. Maintain your control by sitting into a straight-arm bent-wristlock.

4. Sidestep left with lifting-arm-throw.

Sidestep to the left. Move your left arm under your opponent's right arm while bringing your right arm on top. Throw him by stepping around with your right leg while pushing up with your left arm and down with your right. Control your opponent with a kneeling wristlock.

5. Head-push to hair-grab, with face-smash to surfboard.

Step back with your right leg while pushing his head down with both hands. Then kneel on his upper arm, grab his hair, and smash his face into the ground. Maintain control with a double-bent-wrist surfboard.

6. Head shove.

Shove your opponent's head back with both hands.

7. Step-back to arm-wrench-throw.

Step back with your right leg. Hook his left arm with your right arm, pinning it to your side. Throw your opponent by bending down, and control him with a sitting surfboard.

Counters to a Front Single-Leg Takedown from the Tie-up Position

Execute a single-leg takedown by picking up your opponent's ankle while pushing down on his hip or thigh.

1. Neck-crank with wrench, to underarm control, to leg step-over, to head-scissors with reverse full-nelson, to pile-driver.

As your opponent bends to grab your front leg, wrap your left arm around his neck and wrench it by pulling up. Step out with your right leg, while sliding your left leg to the left and placing your right arm under his left. Then step over his head. Your left leg pins his head as you slip your left arm under his right arm. Sit down, driving his head into the ground. Roll him over on his side while scissoring his head.

2. Down-elbow, to forearm-lift-hit, to neck-crank.

As your opponent bends, bring your elbow down on his spine. Grab his chin with your right hand and twist. Then hit him in the neck with your left forearm, and apply a neck-crank by pulling up.

3. Up-knee.

Knee him in the face as he bends down.

Counters to the Single Rear-Leg Pick-up from the Tie-up Position

Here we have a single rear-leg pick-up with a leglock and hair control.

Step behind your opponent. Pick up his right ankle with your right hand. Bring him to the ground by stepping forward with your left leg, while pushing down on the back of his thigh with your left hand. Step over his right leg with your right leg. Get him into a leglock by stepping over him with your left leg and kneeling. Then pull his hair.

1. Adjust position, to leg-buckle-throw, to headlock.

As your opponent attempts to circle behind you, adjust your position so your right leg traps his right leg. Then throw him by kneeling as you step out with your left leg. Sit out and get him in headlock.

2. Adjust position to headlock.

As your opponent attempts to get behind you, adjust your position. Then get him in a headlock and sit out.

3. Chin-throw to forward-neck-crank.

As your opponent attempts to get behind you, grab his chin with both hands and twist, throwing him to the ground. Control him by pushing on his head with your torso.

4. Adjust-position to arm-bar-throw.

As your opponent attempts to get behind you, adjust your position by sliding your left leg back as you grab his left wrist with your left hand. Then bring your opponent to the ground by pulling up on his wrist. At the same time, kneel and push down on his arm with your right forearm. Then sit out into a figure-four arm-bar.

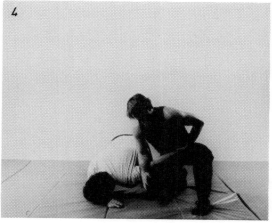

Continued

5. Circle to sitting-leg-lift-throw, to toe-hold leglock.

As your opponent tries to circle behind you, circle to the left and step in front of his right leg with your right leg. Pick up his ankle with both hands. Then sit down into a toe-hold leglock.

Counters to Kali Step-on-Foot, Push-Knee-Throw

To do a kali step-on-foot, push-knee-throw from the tie-up position, pop-up your opponent's right arm with your left palm. Step on his right foot with your right foot, and throw him to the ground by pushing on his knee.

1. Replace step-to-step on foot-push-knee-throw.

As your opponent attempts to step on your foot, step back with your right foot. Then step on his right foot with your left and push him to the ground. Drop your knee on his thigh or groin and control him with a calflock with leg spread.

Continued

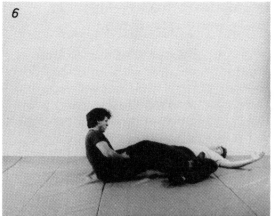

2. Wipe to push-thigh-throw.

After your opponent steps on your foot and starts to push your knee with his right hand, wipe his arm away by hitting it with your left palm. Throw him to the ground by pushing his thigh near the hip. Then kneel on his ankle and get him in a figure-four wristlock.

Continued

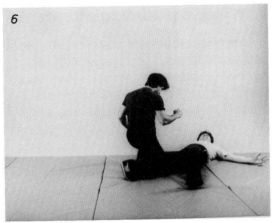

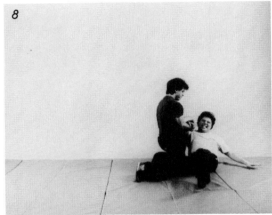

3. Single-leg takedown.

As your opponent steps on your foot, pick up his ankle with your left hand. Throw him to the ground by pushing on his hip. Then stomp on his thigh or groin. Lock his right ankle, then step over him with your left leg and turn him onto his stomach. Execute a leglock by sitting down.

Continued

4. Elbow-and-thigh shove with forearm.

As your opponent steps on your foot, wipe his right arm with your left palm. Then hit his thigh with a horizontal elbow strike and shove him to the ground with your forearm.

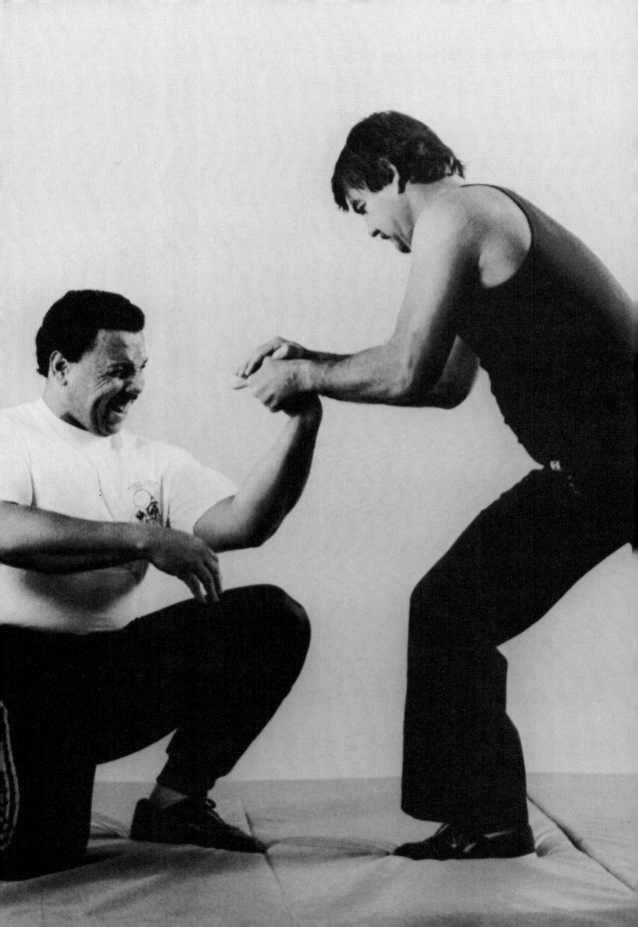

3 The Kali Lock-Flow and Counters to Arm and Wristlocks

Arm and wristlocks are common to many martial arts. They are important, primary techniques in Chin-Na, Jujitsu, and Aikido. In developing Jeet Kune Do, Bruce Lee considered locking to be either accidental or incidental. It's accidental because in JKD, while we don't look for a lock, we may find one. For example, you may slip an opponent's punch, throw an uppercut to the stomach, and get him in a front headlock. It's accidental because it's not planned; it's just there. It's as if your opponent's energy or body position leads him into a lock. Locking in JKD is incidental because it's seldom a primary goal. Locking almost always follows a punch, kick, trap or throw. We believe in softening up an opponent before locking him.

All this is not to say locking is not important. There are times when controlling an opponent may be more important than punching him out. For example, your "opponent" may be a drunk at a party or a mentally disturbed person who may harm himself or others. You may have a job (such as bodyguard, bouncer, or police officer) where controlling an opponent is desired.

This chapter will focus on basic locks and their counters. Keep in mind it would take volumes to do justice to locking alone. With one chapter devoted to locking, we can barely scratch the surface.

The Kali Lock-Flow

Experts in Filipino Kali practice locking by flowing from one lock to another. The flow occurs when you attempt a lock and your opponent resists. When he resists he gives you energy. You flow (or go with) his energy and into another lock. The Kali lock-flow is an example of flowing with your opponent's energy. The lock-flow below is one of countless lock-flows. Many Kali instructors will do a different lock-flow every time they show you an example. This follows the JKD principle of no set pattern, and shows that energy will differ from opponent to opponent. Remember, the lock-flow we will show in this chapter is only one example. Learn it, but don't be bound to it. Once you have learned it, dissolve it, and just go with the flow. Take each lock to where it is defined or set. Stay on the threshold of pain, but don't push past it.

1. Bent-wristlock.

Grab your opponent's right thumb with your left hand. Rotate his hand to the left until his fingers are pointed toward him. Place your right palm on the back of his wrist and push straight down.

2. Cradle.

While holding his right thumb, bring his right arm and grab his right wrist with your right arm and "cradle" it on the crook of your left arm. Then bring your left arm under his right arm and cup it with your left palm on his elbow. Take your right arm and press down with your forearm on his triceps.

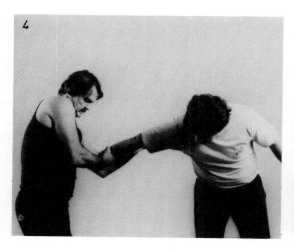

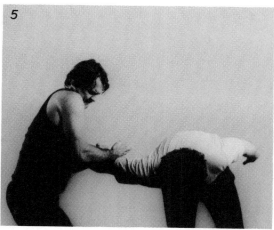

3. Vertical reverse-wristlock.

Keeping control of his right arm, slide your left arm down. Grab his right thumb with your left hand while pressing his hand to your chest. Then bring your right arm under his right arm. With your right palm, slap his right biceps with an upward motion. As you lift up on his biceps, bring his hand down. At the same time, control his upper arm by pressing it against your chest with your right hand.

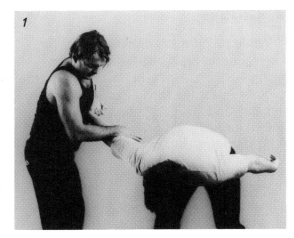

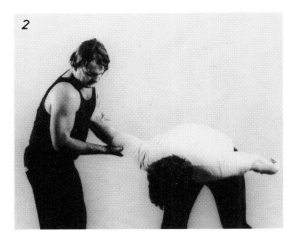

4. Horizontal reverse-wrist-lever come-along.

From the previous position, push down on his upper arm with your right hand. Control your opponent by pressing his elbow into your chest.

5. Finger-grasp with straight-arm-lever.

Reach with your right hand and grasp the first two fingers of his right hand. Pull his arm straight and apply pressure by pulling down on his fingers. At the same time, push up on his elbow with your right palm.

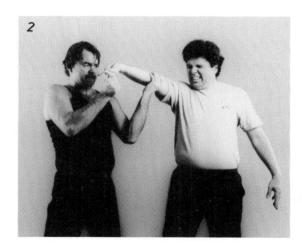

6. Reverse bent-arm wrist-lever.

From the previous position, step to the left and place his elbow on your left shoulder as you grasp his right wrist with your right hand. Bring his arm down so his right hand is parallel to the ground as you grasp all four fingers of his right hand. Apply pressure by twisting his fingers away from your body.

7. Left-hand-insertion to bent-wrist takedown.

From the previous position, grab his right thumb with your left hand. Step up with your left leg. As you rest his forearm on your upper arm, apply pressure by pushing down on his wrist as you pull up on his fingers.

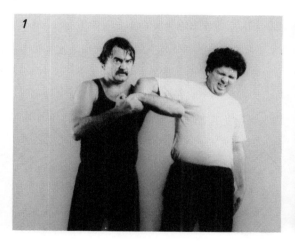

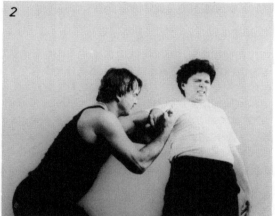

8. Bent-wristlock takedown with forearm pressure.

Hold onto his fingers, while pushing your opponent's arm toward him and releasing his wrist with your left hand. Bring your left arm under his right arm, and place your palm on top of his forearm. Apply pressure by lifting up on the fingers as you push down on his forearm.

9. Forearm takedown.

From the previous position, reach under with your left hand and grab the inside of his forearm. Roll your right hand around until you are grabbing the outside of his wrist. Roll your left arm so your forearm rests on top of his forearm near the elbow. Unbalance your opponent by simultaneously lifting up on his wrist and pushing down on his forearm.

1

2

10. Figure-four wristlock.

Lift up on his right wrist with your right arm. Grasp your right wrist with your left hand. Apply pressure on his wrist by pulling the back of his hand toward you.

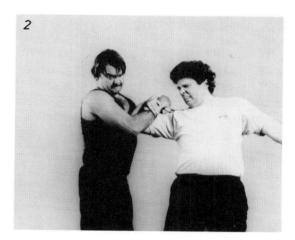

11. Rear-bent-wrist elbow-throw.

While maintaining your grip on his right wrist with your right hand, bring your left hand over the top of your right. Then remove your right hand and apply pressure with your left. Grab his elbow with your right hand and lift.

12. Arm-bar.

Bring his right arm down and grab his wrist with your right hand. Straighten his arm as you place your left forearm on his triceps just above his elbow. The elbow should be pointed toward the sky. Apply pressure by pulling up on his wrist as you push down on his triceps.

13. Underarm-bar.

Rotate his arm as you lift it so his palm is facing up and his elbow down. Support his arm above the elbow on your upper arm near the shoulder. Apply pressure by pulling down on his wrist as you lift up with your left arm.

14. Bent-elbowlock.

Bend his right arm. Then reach under his arm with your right arm and grab his wrist. Apply pressure by pushing down on his wrist as you lift up with your forearm.

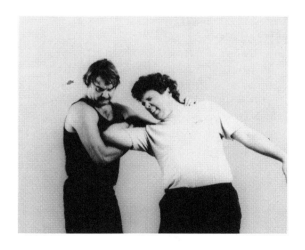

15. Underarm come-along.

Release your grip on his wrist as you reach under his arm with your left arm and pin his forearm to your side. Then grab his elbow with your right hand and grab the back of your right hand with your left. Apply pressure by torquing up.

Once you can do the lock-flow on your training partner's right arm, try it on his left arm. Then make up your own flows. Just flow with the resistance your training partner gives you.

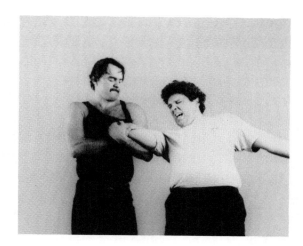

Counters to Wrist and Armlocks

Most of the counters shown below are based on Kali principles. In this section we show some of the ways to dissolve the opponent's lock and reverse it to apply one of our own. A lock must be dissolved before it is defined (see lock-flow). It is usually possible to punch, elbow, knee or head butt before defining the lock. You can also do the above after dissolving the lock. Although strikes are not shown, look at the photos and see where they could fit in.

1. The bent-wristlock.

a. Cut down and shove to straight-arm-bar. As your opponent attempts to get you in a bent-wristlock, chop down on his right wrist with your left palm as you pull your right hand up through his thumb. Then apply a straight-armlock.

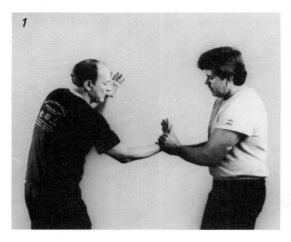
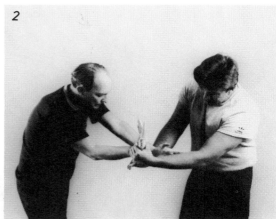
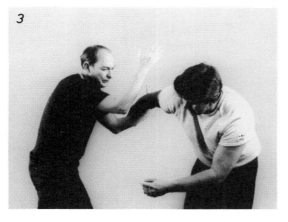

b. Angle and twist his wrist to a bent-wristlock. Another way to counter a bent-wristlock is to angle to the right to relieve the pressure on your wrist as you grab his right hand with your left hand. Then twist his hand and apply a bent-wristlock of your own.

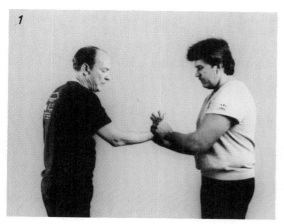

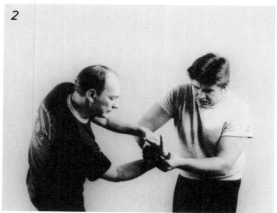

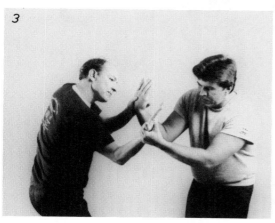

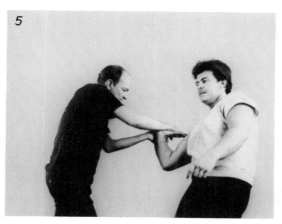

c. Angle-and-twist-wrist to a reverse bent-wristlock. This is the same as "b" except that you grab your opponent's right wrist and apply a reverse bent-wristlock.

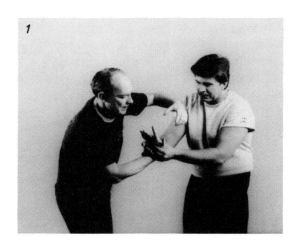

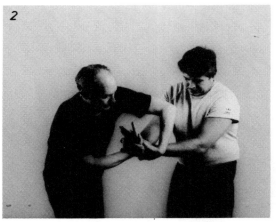

2. The reverse bent-wristlock.

Step-up, to lift-elbow, to armlock. As your opponent attempts to get you in a right reverse bent-wristlock, step up with your left leg. Push up on your opponent's right elbow and apply a right armlock.

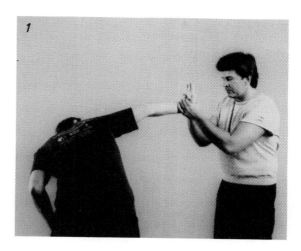

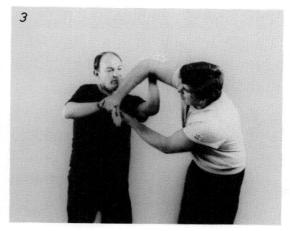

3. Cradle.

Wrap-around come-along. As your opponent attempts a cradlelock, bend his elbow to a wrap-around come-along.

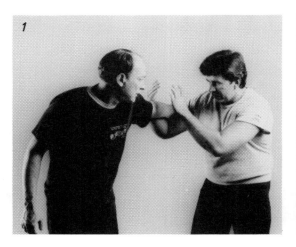 

4. Reverse arm-lever, vertical position.

Up-elbow to bent-wristlock. As your opponent attempts a reverse arm-lever to your left wrist, shove your elbow into his chin by hitting your wrist upward with your right palm. Then apply a two-hand bent-wristlock.

5. Straight-through wristlock with fingers up.

Push on your fingers to a bent-wristlock. To release the wristlock, grab your fingers and push away from your body. Then you can apply a bent-wristlock.

Or you can apply a wrap-around arm-bar.

6. Straight-through wristlock with fingers down.

Push on wrist to bent-wristlock, to finger-squeeze. To release the wristlock, push down on the locked wrist. Then go to a bent wristlock as you squeeze his fingers while stepping back.

7. Finger-grasp with up-arm-bar.

Wipe-brace to wrap-around armlock. To release hold, wipe away the hand under your elbow. Bring your opponent to the ground by shoving down on his forearm with your forearm. Then apply a wrap-around armlock.

8. Reverse wrist-twist.

a. Thumb-grasp to thumblock. As your opponent attempts a reverse wrist-twist and before the lock is defined, grab his thumb and bring him to the ground with a double-hand thumblock.

b. Wipe to finger jab. Or, wipe his arm away to finger jab. (This is one example of hitting after releasing).

9. Underarm-bar.

Shove-elbow to figure-four arm-bar. To release the lock, push on your opponent's elbow with your right palm as you pull back your left arm. Then apply a figure-four arm-bar.

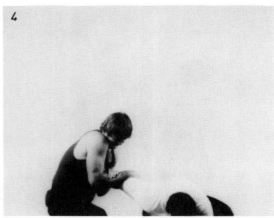

10. Down-arm-bar with handle.

Wipe to down-arm-bar. As opponent starts to apply a down-arm-bar, grab and shove his right wrist (the handle) as you pull your left arm toward your body. Then apply a down-arm-bar.

11. Down-arm-bar without handle.

Wipe and backfist to forearm takedown.
Wipe his brace hand with your right
hand as you pull your arm through his
thumb. Then backfist and take him down
by pushing down on his forearm as you
pull up on his wrist.

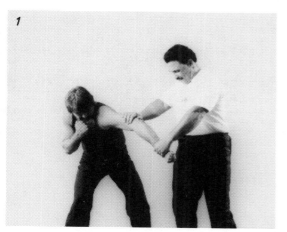

Continued

12. Figure-four wristlock.

Elbow lift to down-arm-bar to figure-four, wristlock takedown to bent-wristlock control. As your opponent attempts a figure-four wristlock, push up on his elbow and apply a down-arm-bar. Stepping out with your right foot, throw him to the ground with a figure-four wristlock. Control him with a bent-wristlock.

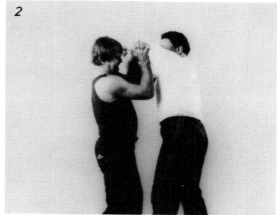

Continued

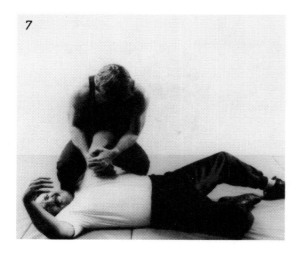

13. Bent-elbow wristlock.

Shove-arm to hammerlock. Before the lock is defined, step out with your left leg as you hit his triceps with your left forearm. Then apply a hammerlock.

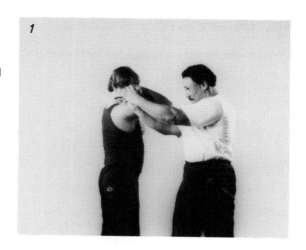

14. Underarm come-along.

Punch-shoulder to shoulder-arm-bar.

15. Over-the-right-shoulder arm-bar.

Chin-twist to headlock. If your opponent is foolish enough to bar your right arm on his right shoulder, twist his neck and apply a headlock.

16. Over-the-left shoulder arm-bar.

Shove-shoulder to reverse-neck-crank.
To release the lock, shove your opponent's shoulder with your left palm as you pull back with your right arm. Grab his chin with your right hand and pivot to your right as you step up with your left leg. Then apply a reverse-neck-crank.

17. Stomach-arm-bar.

Ankle pickup to leg and chinlock.
Reach down and pick up his ankle as
you shove his body forward. Then get
him in a leglock and chin-lift.

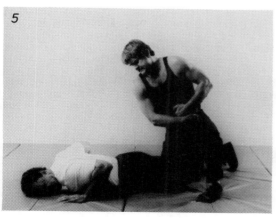

18. Hammerlock.

Backfist, to double-arm wrap-around, to leg pickup, to leglock. Step out with your left leg and backfist. Wrap his arms to your right side. Pick up his ankle and apply a standing leglock.

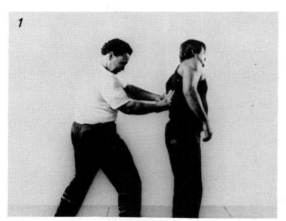

19. Figure-four hammerlock.

Underarm come-along. As your opponent attempts to get you in a figure-four hammerlock, apply an under-arm come-along before the lock is defined.

Many of the techniques in this chapter come from the following Filipino martial artists: Regino Ellustrisino; Juanito Lacosti; Jack Santos; Sam Tendencia; and Floro Villabrille.

4 Counters To Necklocks and Strangles

Side Headlock

From the tie-up position, your opponent gets you in a side headlock.

1. Nose-lift to neck-crank.

Reach over his left shoulder. Place your hand under his nose and pull up. Rotate his body and apply a neck-crank.

2. Nose-lift to leg-lift takedown.

Once you've lifted his nose, throw him by picking up his leg. Then apply a leglock.

3. Leg-buckle.

Before the lock is defined, grab his wrist and buckle his leg by kneeling on it. Then apply an armlock.

Front Neck-Crank

1. Groin-hit to armlock.

To release this lock, grab his wrist and hit his groin with your palm. Slide your left leg back and apply an armlock.

Leg Pickup

Before the lock is defined, pick his leg up as you shove forward with your shoulder. At the same time, step up with your left leg. Then apply a leglock.

Side-Strangle

1. Arm-drag-throw.

From the tie-up position, your opponent attempts an arm pop-up to a side-strangle. Do an arm-drag-throw followed by an elbow and an armlock.

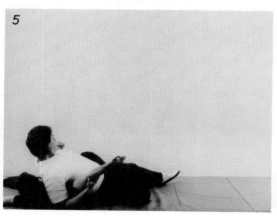

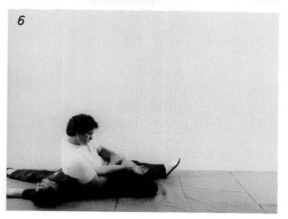

2. Neck-crank.

Same as previous page, but apply a neck-crank.

3. Head-throw.

Same as previous page, but apply a head-lock to neck-crank.

Continued

Rear-Strangle

Getting out of a rear-strangle has more to do with awareness than anything else. You have to get out of the lock before it is defined and your body is bent backward.

1. Elbow to arm-bar takedown.

Grab your opponent's right wrist with your left hand. Bend down and elbow him. Step back with your left leg and duck under his arm. Take him to the ground with a straight-arm-bar. Control him by kneeling on his arm.

Continued

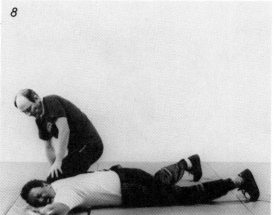

2. Shoulder-throw to figure-four armlock.

Before the lock is defined, throw him with a shoulder-throw and control him with a figure-four armlock.

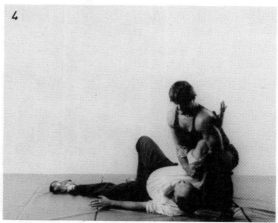

5 Counters to Common Throws

Below are some examples of counters to some of the common throws. These counters may be used before, during and after the throw.

Reaping Throw

Below is an example of a reaping throw.

Counters to the reaping throw

1. Stop-hit (before).

As your opponent gets into range, hit him with a palm-hit to his nose or a finger jab to his eye.

2. Keep a superior position to the reaping throw (during).

As your opponent attempts to throw you, slide your right foot back and throw him.

Then control him with an arm-bar.

3. Cradle throw (during).

As your opponent starts to throw you, step to the left with your left leg. Simultaneously, push his shoulder with your left hand as you scoop his right leg with your right arm. Then throw him by picking him up.

4. Arm-drag-throw to side-strangle (after).

If your opponent throws you, use the momentum for an arm-drag throw. Then control him with a side-strangle.

The Rear-Sweep-Throw

Below is an example of the rear-sweep-throw.

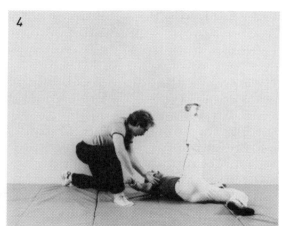

Counters to the rear-sweep-throw

1. Front-reaping-throw.

As your opponent attempts to throw you, grab his right wrist with your left hand and throw him with a front-reaping-throw while pushing down on his head with your right hand. Then control him with an elbowlock.

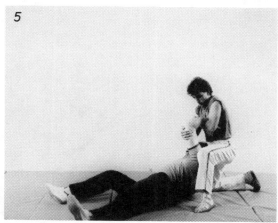

2. Bong sao to arm-bar takedown.

As your opponent comes in for the throw, right bong sao his left arm. Pull your right arm on top of his left and take him to the ground with an arm-bar. Control him with leg-over straight-armlock.

3

4

Front Reaping Throw

Below is an example of a front-reaping-throw with an armlock control.

Counters to the front-reaping-throw

1. Over-arm-hook.

This counter requires great timing, as you have to force your opponent off balance before his leg sweeps you. As he bridges the gap, lock his left arm after it goes over your shoulder. Then bring him to the ground with an armlock.

Continued

2. Leg-lift to front-reaping-throw.

As your opponent tries to reap you, lift your front leg and reap him. Then control him with an armlock.

3. Tackle, to leg-buckle, to leglock with chin-lift.

As your opponent bridges the gap, shove his chest with your right forearm, and grab his left leg with your left arm. Throw him to the ground by pushing forward as you buckle his right leg with your right leg. Then roll him over and apply a leglock with chin-lift.

Shoulder Throw

Below is an example of a shoulder throw.

Counters to the shoulder throw

1. Hip-push to rear choke.

As your opponent comes in to throw you, push him off balance by shoving his hip. Then apply a rear choke.

2. Step-over to rear hip-throw.

As your opponent comes in to throw you, push on his back. Step in front of his left leg with your right as you bring your right arm across his throat and throw him with a rear hip-throw. Then control him with a choke.

The Hip Throw

Below is an example of a hip throw.

Counters to the hip throw

1. Arm-across-throat to cradle-throw.

As your opponent starts to turn his back on you, step up with your left leg. Then throw him with a cradle-throw.

2. Up-elbow, to front choke, to circle-throw.

As your opponent steps out, and before he turns his back, hit him with an up-elbow strike. Get him in a front choke and throw him with a circle-throw. Continue the choke when you're both on the ground.

3. Chin-twist, to leg-buckle, to leglock.

As your opponent turns to throw you, stop his movement by twisting his chin as you step up with your left leg. Bring him to the ground by buckling his leg. Then get him in a leglock.

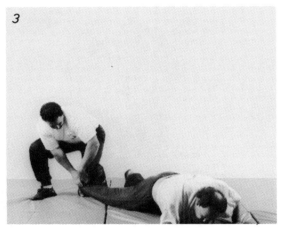

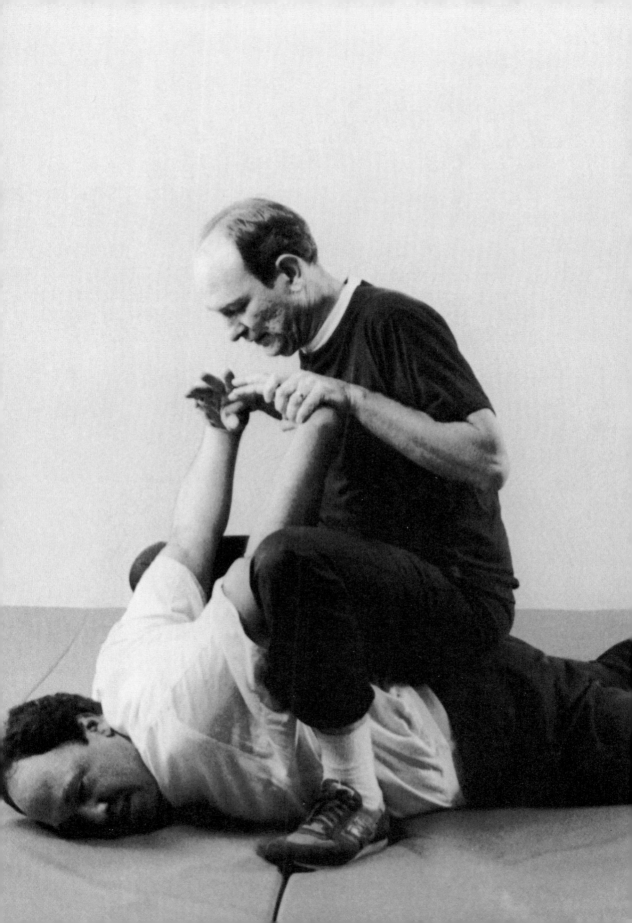

6 Groundfighting

It is important to learn how to fight when you're on the ground. No matter how good a boxer or kicker you are, the time may come when you're knocked down, or your opponent may tie you up and throw you. If you've seen many streetfights you know in most cases both fighters end up on the ground. The one-punch or one-kick knockout usually occurs only in movies.

Both on the ground

1. On your back.

A position not as bad as it looks is on your back with your opponent on top of you. In this example, your opponent is choking you.

a. Pull him to you, to side-strangle.
Bend your opponent's right arm with your left as you reach around his head. Then twist his chin and apply a strangle.

You can also roll him over and apply a leg- and neck-hold.

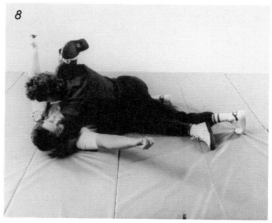

b. Hair-pull with chin-twist. Bend his right elbow with your right hand. Pull his hair with your left hand. At the same time, twist his chin with your right and pull him toward you. Then roll him over and apply an armlock with your legs as you strangle him.

c. Pressure points. This position allows easy access to various pressure points. Remember, when your life is at stake, there's no such thing as dirty fighting.

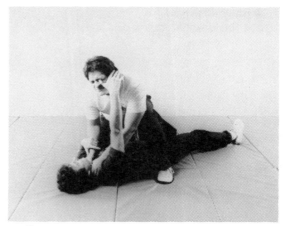

1. Eye gouge.

2. Thumb to the brachial plexus nerve.

3. Armpit peck-pinch.

4. Triceps pinch.

5. Groin grab.

d. Armlock throw.

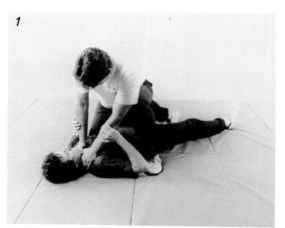

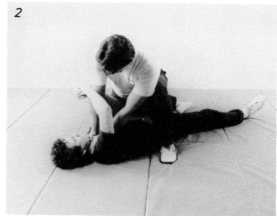

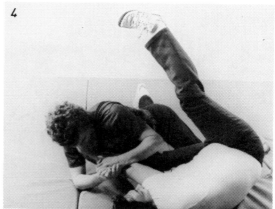

e. Knee to spine.

If your opponent is on your upper torso, you can throw him by kneeing his spine and rolling. Then grab his arm and control him with an armlock.

2. On your side.

a. Roll to the left with leg-lift to double-leglock with scissors. Roll to your left as you pick up his left leg.

Then apply a single-leglock.
Or a double-leglock with scissors.

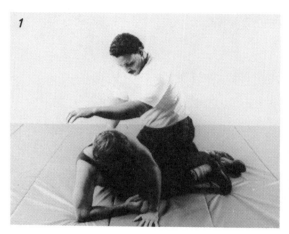

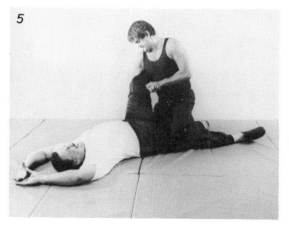

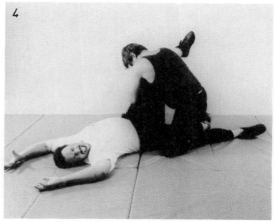

b. Roll to the right to wristlock. Roll to the right as you push down on his arm. At the same time, shove his chest with your elbow. Then apply a wristlock as you kneel on his neck.

c. Grab leg and roll. If your opponent is in a position where you can grab his leg, do so and roll. Then apply a leglock.

3. On your hands and knees.

Roll to your left while lifting with your left arm.

4. On your stomach.

a. Roll to the left with armlock. If your opponent is on your left side, roll to your left and apply an armlock.

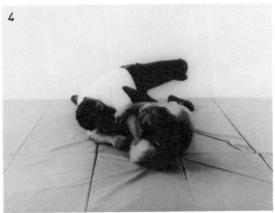

b. Roll to finger-break. This position is one of the worst to be in.

It may be possible to roll and release the choke by grabbing and breaking a finger.

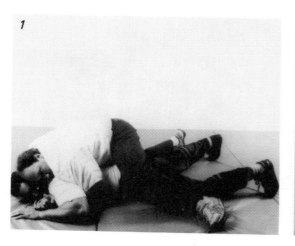

You're on the Ground while Your Opponent is Standing

There is a lot you can do from this position. In fact, many Indonesian Pentjak Silat fighters prefer this position. Below are some of the attacks possible from this position.

a. Roll and right-side kick.

b. Roll and left-side kick.

c. Right leg behind right ankle, with left-side kick to knee.

d. Left leg behind right ankle, to right-side kick to knee.

e. Right foot behind left ankle, with left-side kick to knee.

About the Authors

Larry Hartsell

According to Dan Inosanto, Larry Hartsell is among the world's premier jeet kune do fighters. Larry started his martial arts training by studying judo in North Carolina from 1957-1960. Shortly after receiving his black belt in kenpo, he went into the Army, serving in Vietnam from 1966-1967. After his discharge from the Army, Larry was fortunate enough to study jeet kune do from Bruce Lee and Dan Inosanto from 1967-1970. When he moved back to North Carolina in 1973, Larry opened the only authorized jeet kune do school east of California.

Larry has an associate degree in criminology, and ten years of practical experience in law enforcement. He also has had extensive training in boxing and wrestling. Besides teaching in his own school, Larry has taught self-defense tactics and baton to law enforcement officers at Piedmont Central Community College and has worked with the Dallas Cowboys and San Francisco 49ers. He has taught at the California Martial Arts Academy at the University of California at Irvine. For the last two summers, he and Tim Tackett have taught at the Great Smoky Mountain JKD/Kali/Thai Camp in Brasstown, North Carolina.

Tim Tackett

From 1962-1965, Tim Tackett studied Chinese boxing in Taiwan with both the Mainland Chinese and Native Taiwanese Boxing associations. While in Taiwan, Tackett studied *Hsing-I, Kung-Fu, Chin Na, Tai Chi,* and both Northern and Southern Shaolin boxing. An early "backyard" student of Dan Inosanto, Tackett is a graduate of the Filipino Kali Academy. He has an Associate Instructor's Certificate in the *Jun Fan* arts and *Eskrima.*

Tackett restricts his formal teaching to a few backyard students and to occasional seminars around the country. An innovator in adapting JKD principles to football, he has worked with the Dallas Cowboys and San Francisco 49ers.

Tackett is the author of two books on hsing-I kung-fu. He is the co-author with Chris Kent of *The Kickboxing Aspects of Jeet Kune Do*, and the co-author with Larry Hartsell of *Jeet Kune Do: Entering to Trapping to Grappling*.

Married and the father of two children, Tackett earned a master's degree in drama from the University of California at Riverside, where he graduated Phi Beta Kappa. He is now an English and drama teacher at Montclair High School in Montclair, California.

UNIQUE LITERARY BOOKS OF THE WORLD

Also publishers of:
Inside Karate
Inside Kung-Fu

UNIQUE PUBLICATIONS
4201 Vanowen Place
Burbank, CA 91505

PLEASE WRITE IN
FOR OUR LATEST CATALOG